Understanding the CPI

Imagine this: you go to the grocery store one day and buy a loaf of bread for $2.

The next month, you go back to buy the same loaf of bread, but now it costs $2.10.

You might think, "Why did the price increase? Is it just this store or is it happening everywhere?" This is where the CPI comes into play.

The CPI is a measure that examines the weighted average of prices of a basket of consumer goods and services, such as transportation, food, and medical care.

Essentially, it tracks how the prices of these goods and services change over time.

The Importance of CPI

Now, you might wonder, why should we care about tracking the prices of these everyday items? Well, the CPI serves several crucial purposes:

1. **Inflation Measurement**:
 One of the primary uses of CPI is to measure inflation. Inflation refers to the rate at which the general level of prices for goods and services is rising, eroding purchasing power. By tracking changes in the CPI over time, economists and policymakers can gauge the rate of inflation in the economy.

2. **Economic Indicator:**

 CPI serves as a key economic indicator.

 It provides insights into the overall health of the economy.

 High inflation rates can indicate overheating in the economy, while low or negative inflation rates might signal economic slowdown or recession.

3. Cost-of-Living Adjustment (COLA):

Many contracts, including labor contracts, pensions, and Social Security benefits, are indexed to the CPI.

This means that when the CPI rises, these payments increase to maintain the purchasing power of recipients.

4. **Monetary Policy**:

Central banks, such as the Federal Reserve in the United States, use CPI data to make monetary policy decisions.

If inflation is rising too quickly, the central bank may decide to raise interest rates to cool down the economy.

Conversely, if inflation is too low, they may lower interest rates to stimulate economic activity.

5. Investment Decision Making:

Investors also pay attention to CPI data.

Rising inflation can erode the real returns on investments, particularly fixed-income assets like bonds.

Understanding CPI trends can help investors adjust their portfolios accordingly.

How CPI is Calculated

Now, let's talk about how the CPI is calculated. The process involves several steps:

1. **Selecting the Basket of Goods:**

The first step is to determine the basket of goods and services that will be included in the CPI.

This basket represents the typical consumption patterns of urban households.

2. **Collecting Price Data:**

Government agencies, such as the Bureau of Labor Statistics (BLS) in the United States, collect price data for the items in the basket at regular intervals.

This data is collected from various sources, including retail stores, service providers, and online retailers.

3. **Weighting the Items:**

Not all items in the basket have the same importance in consumers' budgets.

For example, housing expenses typically have a higher weight than entertainment expenses.

Therefore, each item is assigned a weight based on its relative importance.

4. **Calculating the Index:**

 Once the price data and weights are collected, the CPI is calculated using a formula that takes into account the price changes for each item and their respective weights.

 The result is an index number that represents the overall change in prices.

5. Seasonal Adjustment:

Some items may have seasonal variations in prices, such as fruits and vegetables.

To account for this, seasonal adjustments may be applied to the CPI data.

6. **Publishing the CPI:**

The final CPI number is published regularly, usually monthly or quarterly, depending on the country.

This allows economists, policymakers, businesses, and the public to track inflation trends over time.

Using CPI for Financial Success

Now, let's talk about how you can use CPI data to achieve financial success:

1. **Budgeting:**

CPI data can help you anticipate changes in the cost of living. By understanding how prices are trending, you can adjust your budget accordingly. For example, if CPI data suggests that food prices are rising, you might allocate more money to your grocery budget.

2. **Investment Strategy:**

Investors can use CPI data to inform their investment decisions.

Inflation can have a significant impact on investment returns, particularly for fixed-income securities like bonds.

If CPI data indicates rising inflation, investors may consider allocating more of their portfolio to assets that tend to perform well during inflationary periods, such as stocks or real estate.

3. **Negotiating Contracts:**

If you're entering into a contract that includes cost-of-living adjustments, such as a salary negotiation or a lease agreement, understanding CPI trends can give you valuable information for negotiation.

For example, if CPI has been rising consistently, you may want to negotiate for a higher salary or a lower rent increase.

4. **Debt Management:**

Rising inflation can erode the purchasing power of money over time.

If you have debt with a fixed interest rate, such as a mortgage or student loan, inflation can work in your favor by reducing the real value of your debt. However, if you have debt with a variable interest rate, like credit card debt, rising inflation could mean higher interest payments. Understanding CPI trends can help you make informed decisions about managing your debt.

5. **Retirement Planning:**

For retirees, maintaining purchasing power is crucial.

Social Security benefits and pensions often include cost-of-living adjustments tied to CPI.

By staying informed about CPI trends, retirees can better plan for their financial future and ensure that their income keeps pace with inflation.

Conclusion

In summary, the Consumer Price Index (CPI) is a vital economic indicator that measures changes in the prices of a basket of consumer goods and services over time.

It serves multiple purposes, including inflation measurement, economic indicator, and indexation for contracts and investments.

Understanding CPI data and trends can empower individuals to make informed financial decisions, whether it's budgeting, investing, negotiating contracts, managing debt, or planning for retirement.

By leveraging CPI data, individuals can navigate the dynamic economic landscape and work towards achieving financial success.

Please use the next few pages for your notes and debates.

www.ingramcontent.com/pod-product-compliance
Lightning Source LLC
Chambersburg PA
CBHW030105230526
45471CB00003B/1265